Memory Lane through the Mirror

Skylar Dopp

BookLeaf Publishing

India | USA | UK

Memory Lane through the Mirror © 2021
Skylar Dopp

All rights reserved.

Presentation by *BookLeaf Publishing*

Web: www.bookleafpub.com

E-mail: info@bookleafpub.com

ISBN: 9789357448413

First edition 2021

DEDICATION

for all those who believed in me when I did not
believe in myself

ACKNOWLEDGEMENT

I want to thank Book Leaf Publishing for giving me this opportunity I also want to thank all my friends and family who listened to me update them whenever Imade progress on the book, and who encouraged me to never let the writing feel forced, and guided me to create a book I love.

PREFACE

i wish all my readers strength in their future healing, and acceptance and love to their past self.

AM I MYSELF IF I AM ALSO EVERYONE ELSE

Never been exceptional with a compass
Never assured on the way to go
No decipher between what I truly desire
Is it what I want
Or is it a bullet on a list
I made for someone long ago.

THE INNER CHILD IS NOT A CRITIQUE

The girl in the mirror peers into me
I observe an inflated face
Avert my eye contact
All i can view is the back of her head
Little hands stretch forward
Her pinky finger barely holding on
Enclosed in a raggedy red string
attached to the girl's shaky hand
She pleads with me to stop
The pieces do not come back whole
Soon i will have to go
You will lose me
If you continue to treat me this way
If you critique everything about a woman
Only a girl who has no love for herself will stay

SAVING MY BREATH

3

I tear my fingers into coarse skin
I beg you to stay
simultaneously
forcing you to walk out the door
Begging for someone to stay
Because when they left
I questioned why i breathe
When the whole time i should be questioning
Why did I believe they were worth my breath?

THE RAGE

4

I locked it away
While it demanded to be felt
If i cannot feel it
Neither can you.
Why are you mad?
Just cry like i do.
My observations infuriate me
I deny the existence
Feelings are valid
But not the anger.

THEY ARE NOT YOUR
BURDEN TO CARRY

Anyone who believes
They are
above you
trust they are
below you
In the deepest parts of their mind
and you
do not need to carry their pain
It is
heavy enough
They are not willing to bear it themselves.

AND SOMETIMES IT DOES

6

yesterday they were a stranger
today you have to remember them until you
forget

Only If you forget

Sometimes time does not heal.

WHO COULD LOVE A WEED

Thistles bordering my vacant hands
Throbbing pain throughout my body
I already knew
I wish I could tell you about
The red shovel
The absence of the sun
the irony in the tinted yellow wood
And the thief in my daydreams
Instead I'll mention
The morning glory.

TIME TRAVELING

The story in the silence

It is so loud

Eye contact met with memories that were never made

We had a little longer to go

SEASON GREETINGS

It was dead grass
it was playground toys being put away to avoid
destruction
Lightly damaging the innocence of the children
Lust carried In strong gusts
Loneliness on the tongue
An aggressive foreshadowing

I AM SORRY

im sorry the first time we meet
I will see footprints

Not crafted by your shoe

WHO WINS

11

Dolled up for the chilling night
Decorated head to toe in a light shade
Another Displays a cape
Whereas for a blind man it is just Dark

BEFRIENDING MYSELF

12

Screaming in my mind was no longer efficient
It had to be spoken
I AM INTELLIGENT
I AM BEAUTIFUL
I AM WORTHY OF LOVE
I Always have been.

YOU WON'T HEAL WHAT YOU DROWN

Understand healing is not linear
Even something as beautiful as the ocean at time
recedes.

5'8

I have stood at four inches the majority of life
 I Was tired of needing a ladder to see the sky
I never before requested to measure
Or inquired why
I had no desire to gain knowledge
of how this came to be
I linger in my tiny form.
When i was stomped on
 It was not just,
Nor fair
I did nothing to change it
But i could not care

I now stand much taller and i can see
After putting in the work
The only one who could have helped me
has always been me

ALLOW YOURSELF TO BE NEW

Self love is not always pretty
No simplicity in it
Everyday must be new
And yesterday's mistakes
Must die with the sunset
They will swallow you whole

THROUGH THE MIRROR

I picture the world
No one is whole

I will grow old before i can repair
What does not want to be fixed.

FOR ME

17

Even in the blackest of holes i always find love
I have been conditioning myself not to

LOVING EVERYONE IS NOT A BAD THING
(but do not ruin yourself trying to make
everyone see love in you)

LOVE NEVER HURT

18

at what point in the decipher of what love is not
do you stop translating and allow it to be what it
is

TO FEEL SOMETHING

19

Your lungs ache from the noise
you have tried everything
To feel something

You have not allowed yourself feeling
Self deleterious habits will not heal you.

What are you looking for ?

YOU ARE NOT CHAOS

20

Never had order in your mind
Your thoughts never collective
You live in your head of disarray
Still,
you are not chaos

DREAM RAIN

21

The clouds are gray
The rain falls on my face
I jump in the puddles
`I jump into the clouds
The birds go by
Goodbye rain I hope you come back
another day
Goodbye goodbye goodbye

-kd